Born in 2000

by

Kerry Butters.

Born in 2000

Millennium:	2nd millennium
Centuries:	19th century – **20th century** – 21st century
Decades:	1970s 1980s 1990s – **2000s** – 2010s 2020s 2030s
Years:	1997 1998 1999 – **2000** – 2001 2002 2003

2000 (MM) was a century leap year starting on Saturday (dominical letter BA) of the Gregorian calendar, the 2000th year of the Common Era (CE) and *Anno Domini* (AD) designations, the 1000th and last year of the 2nd millennium, the 100th and last year of the 20th century, and the 1st year of the 2000s decade.

2000 was designated as:

- International Year for the Culture of Peace
- World Mathematical Year

Popular culture holds the year 2000 as the first year of the 21st century and the 3rd millennium due to a tendency of grouping the years according to decimal values, as if year zero were counted. According to the Gregorian Calendar, these distinctions fall to the year 2001 because the 1st century was retroactively said to start with year AD 1. Since the calendar does not have year zero, its first millennium spanned from years 1 to 1000 inclusively and its second millennium from years 1001 to 2000 (See more at *Millennium*).

The year 2000 is sometimes abbreviated as "Y2K" (the "Y" stands for "year", and the "K" stands for "kilo" which means "thousand"). The year 2000 was the subject of Y2K concerns, which are fears that computers would not shift from 1999 to 2000 correctly. However, by the end of 1999, many companies had already converted to new, or upgraded, existing software. Some even obtained *Y2K certification*. As a result of massive effort, relatively few problems occurred.

Contents

Events

January

- January 1 – The piece Longplayer begins. It lasts 1,000 years, finishing on December 31, 2999.
- January 3–10 – Israel and Syria hold inconclusive peace talks.
- January 5–8 – The 2000 al-Qaeda Summit of several high-level al-Qaeda members (including 2 9/11 American Airlines hijackers) is held in Kuala Lumpur, Malaysia.
- January 6 – The last natural Pyrenean ibex is found dead, apparently killed by a falling tree.
- January 10 – America Online announces an agreement to purchase Time Warner for $162 billion (the largest-ever corporate merger).
- January 11 – The armed wing of the Islamic Salvation Front concludes its negotiations with the government for an amnesty and disbands in Algeria (see Algerian Civil War#GIA destroyed, GSPC discontinues).
- January 14
    - A United Nations tribunal sentences 5 Bosnian Croats to up to 25 years in prison for the 1993 killing of over 100 Bosnian Muslims in a Bosnian village.
    - The Dow Jones Industrial Average closes at 11,722.98 (at the peak of the Dot-com bubble).
- January 18 – The Tagish Lake meteorite impacts the Earth.
- January 24 – God's Army, a Karen militia group led by twins Johnny and Luther Htoo, takes 700 hostages at a Thai hospital near the Burmese border.

- January 30 – Kenya Airways Flight 431 crashes off the coast of Ivory Coast into the Atlantic Ocean, killing 169.
- January 31
  - Alaska Airlines Flight 261 crashes off the California coast into the Pacific Ocean, killing 88.
  - Dr. Harold Shipman is found guilty of murdering 15 patients between 1998 at Hyde, Greater Manchester, and sentenced to life imprisonment.

February

- February 4 – German extortionist Klaus-Peter Sabotta is jailed for life for attempted murder and extortion, in connection with the sabotage of German railway lines.
- February 6 – Tarja Halonen is elected the first female president of Finland.
- February 7 – Stipe Mesić is elected president of Croatia.
- February 8 – Radio broadcaster Bob Collins' plane collides with that of a student pilot over Zion, Illinois.
- February 9 – Torrential rains in Africa lead to the worst flooding in Mozambique in 50 years, which lasts until March and kills 800 people.
- February 13 – The final original *Peanuts* comic strip is published, following the death of its creator, Charles M. Schulz.
- February 21 – UNESCO holds the inaugural celebration of International Mother Language Day.
- February 29 – a rare century leap year date occurs. Usually, 00 years are not leap years due to not being exactly divisible by 400. 2000 is the first such year to have a February 29 since the year 1600, making it only the second such occasion since leap years were introduced in the late 16th century. The next such leap year will not occur until 2400.

March

- March 1
  - The Constitution of Finland is rewritten.
  - Jorge Batlle, a son, grandnephew and great-grandson of former presidents, is sworn in as President of Uruguay.
- March 4 – The PlayStation 2 is released in Japan. Several months later, it becomes the best-selling game console of all time.
- March 8 – Tokyo train disaster: A sideswipe collision of 2 Tokyo Metro trains kills 5 people.
- March 10 – The NASDAQ Composite Index reaches an all-time high of 5,048. Two weeks later, the NASDAQ-100, S&P 500, and Wilshire 5000 reach their peaks prior to the Dot-com bubble, ending a bull market run that lasted over 17 years.
- March 12
  - Pope John Paul II apologizes for the wrongdoings by members of the Roman Catholic Church throughout the ages.
  - A Zenit-3SL launch fails due to a software bug.
- March 13 – The United States dollar becomes the official currency of Ecuador, replacing the Ecuadorian sucre.
- March 21
  - Pope John Paul II begins the first official visit by a Roman Catholic pontiff to Israel Just Like a 1994.
  - The U.S. Supreme Court rules the FDA lacks authority to regulate tobacco as an addictive drug, throwing out the Clinton Administration's main anti-smoking initiative.
- March 26
  - Vladimir Putin is elected President of Russia.
  - The Seattle Kingdome is demolished by implosion.
- March 27 – The Phillips explosion of 2000 kills 1 and injures 71 in Pasadena, Texas.
- March 28 – A tornado hits Fort Worth, Texas, damaging the downtown area.

April

- April 1 – The 2000 United States Census begins. 281,421,906 residents are living in the United States.
- April 3 – *United States v. Microsoft Corp.*: Microsoft is ruled to have violated United States antitrust laws by keeping "an oppressive thumb" on its competitors.
- April 16 – An American anti-globalization protest is held in Washington, D.C.
- April 17 – Tuanku Syed Sirajuddin becomes Raja of Perlis.
- April 22 – In a predawn raid, federal agents seize 6-year-old Elián González from his relatives' home in Miami and fly him to his Cuban father in Washington, D.C., ending one of the most publicized custody battles in U.S. history.
- April 30 – Canonization of Faustina Kowalska in the presence of 200,000 people and the first Divine Mercy Sunday celebrated worldwide.

May

- May – Sierra Leone Civil War: The British Armed Forces launch Operation Palliser to support the Sierra Leone government to counter the Revolutionary United Front.
- May 1 – A new class of composite material is fabricated, which has a combination of physical properties never before seen in a natural or man-made material.
- May 3 – In San Antonio, Texas, computer pioneer Datapoint files for Chapter 11 bankruptcy.
- May 4
  - After originating in the Philippines, the ILOVEYOU computer virus spreads quickly throughout the world.
  - An earthquake hits Banggai, Indonesia, leaving 54 dead.
- May 5 – A rare conjunction of 7 celestial bodies (Sun, Moon, planets Mercury–Saturn) occurs during the new moon.
- May 11
  - The billionth living person in India is born.

- o Effective date of Canada's first modern-day treaty – The Nisga'a Final Agreement.
- May 12 – The Tate Modern Gallery opens in London.
- May 13
  - o A fireworks factory disaster in Enschede, Netherlands, kills 23.
  - o Millennium Force opens at Cedar Point amusement park in Sandusky, Ohio as the world's tallest and fastest roller coaster.
- May 16 – The Grand National Assembly of Turkey elects Ahmet Necdet Sezer as the tenth President of Turkey.
- May 17 – A bomb in Glorietta Mall in Makati City, Philippines injures 13.
- May 20 – Taiwanese (ROC) president Chen Shui-bian makes the Four Noes and One Without pledge to Taiwan.
- May 25 – Israel withdraws IDF forces from southern Lebanon after 22 years.

June

- June 4 – The 7.9 Mw Enggano earthquake shakes southwestern Sumatra with a maximum Mercalli intensity of VI (*Strong*). One-hundred and three people were killed and 2,174–2,585 were injured.
- June 5 – *405 The Movie*, the first short film widely distributed on the Internet, is released.
- June 13 – South Korean President Kim Dae-jung visits North Korea to participate in the first North-South presidential summit.
- June 17 – A centennial earthquake (6.5 on the Richter scale) hits Iceland on its national day.
- June 21 – Section 28, a law preventing the promotion of homosexuality, is repealed by the Scottish Parliament.
- June 26 – A preliminary draft of genomes, as part of the Human Genome Project, is finished. It is announced at the White House by President Clinton.
- June 28 – Elián González returns to Cuba with his father, Juan Miguel González, ending a protracted custody battle.

- June 30 – At the Roskilde Festival near Copenhagen, Denmark, 9 die and 26 are injured on a set while the rock group Pearl Jam performs.

July

- July 1 – Øresund Bridge between Denmark and Sweden opens.
- July 2
  - France defeats Italy 2-1 after extra time in the final of the European Championships, becoming the first team to win the World Cup and European Championships consecutively.
  - Vicente Fox is elected President of Mexico, as candidate of the rightist PAN (National Action Party), ending 71 years of PRI (Institutional Revolutionary Party) rule.
- July 10
  - In southern Nigeria, a leaking petroleum pipeline explodes, killing about 250 villagers who were scavenging gasoline.
  - Bashar al-Assad is confirmed as Syria's leader in a national referendum following the death of his father, Hafez al-Assad.
- July 13–25 – Israel's prime minister Ehud Barak and PLO leader Yasser Arafat meet at Camp David, but fail to reach an agreement.
- July 14 – A powerful solar flare, later named the Bastille Day event, causes a geomagnetic storm on Earth.
- July 18 – Alex Salmond resigns as the leader of the Scottish National Party.
- July 21–23 – G-8 Nations hold their 26th Annual Summit; issues include AIDS, the 'digital divide', and halving world poverty by 2015.
- July 25 – Air France Flight 4590, a Concorde aircraft, crashes into a hotel in Gonesse just after takeoff from Paris, killing all 109 aboard and 4 in the hotel.
- July 30 – Venezuela's president Hugo Chávez is reelected with 59% of the vote.
- July 31 – August 3 – The Republican National Convention in Philadelphia nominates Governor of Texas George W. Bush for President of the United States and Dick Cheney for Vice President.

August

- August 3 – Rioting erupts on the Paulsgrove estate in Portsmouth, Hampshire, England, after more than 100 people besiege the home of a block of flats allegedly housing a convicted paedophile. This is the latest vigilante violence against suspected sex offenders since the beginning of the "naming and shaming" anti-paedophile campaign by the tabloid newspaper *News of the World*.
- August 7 – DeviantART is launched.
- August 8 – The Confederate submarine *H. L. Hunley* is raised to the surface after 136 years on the ocean floor.
- August 12 – The Russian submarine *Kursk* sinks in the Barents Sea during one of the largest Russian naval exercises since the 1991 dissolution of the Soviet Union, resulting in the deaths of all 118 men on board.
- August 14
    - Tsar Nicholas II and his family are canonized by the synod of the Russian Orthodox Church.
    - *Dora the Explorer*, one of Nickelodeon's most popular shows, debuts.
- August 14–17 – The Democratic National Convention in Los Angeles nominates U.S. Vice President Al Gore for President and Senator Joe Lieberman for Vice President.
- August 23 – John Anthony Kaiser, a Roman Catholic priest, is murdered in Morendat, Kenya.
- August 24 – The Nintendo GameCube is revealed.

September

- September 5 – Tuvalu joins the United Nations.
- September 6 – The last wholly Swedish-owned arms manufacturer, Bofors, is sold to American arms manufacturer United Defense.
- September 6–8 – World leaders attend the Millennium Summit at U.N. Headquarters.
- September 7–14 – The UK fuel protests take place, with refineries blockaded, and supply to the country's network of petrol stations halted.

- September 8
  - Albania officially joins the World Trade Organization.
  - The United Nations Millennium Declaration is made in New York.
- September 13 – Steve Jobs introduces the public beta of Mac OS X for US$29.95.
- September 15 – October 1 – The 2000 Summer Olympics are held in Sydney, Australia.
- September 16
  - Ukrainian journalist Georgiy Gongadze is last seen alive; this day is taken as the commemoration date of his death.
  - Peru's president Alberto Fujimori calls for new elections in which he will not run.
- September 26
  - The Greek ferry *Express Samina* sinks off the coast of the island of Paros; 80 out of a total of over 500 passengers perish in one of Greece's worst sea disasters.
  - Anti-globalization protests in Prague (some 15,000 protesters) turn violent during the IMF and World Bank summits.
- September 28 – Israeli opposition leader Ariel Sharon visits the Temple Mount, protected by a several-hundred-strong Israeli police force. Palestinian riots erupt, leading to a full-fledged armed uprising (called the Al-Aqsa Intifada by sympathizers and the Oslo War by opponents).
- September 29 – The HM Prison Maze in Northern Ireland is closed.

October

- October 1 – The 2000 Summer Olympics close in Sydney, Australia.
- October 5 – President Slobodan Milošević leaves office after widespread demonstrations throughout Serbia.
- October 6 – The last Mini is produced in Longbridge.
- October 11
  - Jim Wallace becomes Acting First Minister of Scotland.

- o 250 million US gallons (950,000 m^3) of coal sludge spill in Martin County, Kentucky (considered a greater environmental disaster than the Exxon Valdez oil spill).
- October 12 – In Aden, Yemen, USS *Cole* is badly damaged by two Al-Qaeda suicide bombers, who place a small boat laden with explosives alongside the United States Navy destroyer, killing 17 crew members and wounding at least 39.
- October 21 – Fifteen Arab leaders convene in Cairo, Egypt, for their first summit in 4 years; the Libyan delegation walks out, angry over signs the summit will stop short of calling for breaking ties with Israel.
- October 22 – The *Mainichi Shimbun* newspaper exposes Japanese archeologist Shinichi Fujimura as a fraud; Japanese archaeologists had based their treatises on his findings.
- October 23 – Madeleine Albright holds talks with North Korean dictator Kim Jong-il.
- October 26 – Pakistani authorities announce that their police have found an apparently ancient mummy of a Persian Princess in the province of Balochistan. Iran, Pakistan and the Taliban all claim the mummy until Pakistan announces it is a modern-day fake on April 17, 2001.
- October 27
  - o Pacific Islands Forum (PIF).
  - o Henry McLeish becomes First Minister of Scotland.
- October 30 – This is the final date during which there is no human presence in space; on October 31, Soyuz TM-31 launches, carrying the first resident crew to the International Space Station. The ISS has been continuously crewed since.
- October 31 – Singapore Airlines Flight 006 collides with construction equipment in the Chiang Kai Shek International Airport, resulting in 83 deaths.

November

- November – Iraq disarmament crisis: Iraq rejects new U.N. Security Council weapons inspections proposals.

- November 1 - Serbia is admitted to the United Nations as the 190th member.
- November 2 – The first resident crew enters the International Space Station.
- November 3 – Widespread flooding occurs throughout England and Wales after days of heavy rain.
- November 7
    - In London, a criminal gang raids the Millennium Dome to steal the Millennium Star diamond, but police surveillance catches them in the act.
    - Hillary Rodham Clinton is elected to the United States Senate, becoming the first First Lady of the United States to win public office.
    - United States presidential election, 2000: Republican Governor of Texas George W. Bush defeats Democratic Vice President Al Gore in the U.S. presidential election but there is a miscount in Florida resulting in a recount of the votes.
- November 11 – Kaprun disaster, Austria: A funicular fire in an Alpine tunnel kills 155 skiers and snowboarders.
- November 15 – A new Indian state called Jharkhand is formed, carving out the South Chhota Nagpur area from Bihar in India.
- November 16 – Bill Clinton becomes the first sitting U.S. President to visit Vietnam since the end of the Vietnam War in 1975.
- November 17
    - A catastrophic landslide in Log pod Mangartom, Slovenia, kills 7, and causes millions of SIT of damage. It is one of the worst catastrophes in Slovenia in the past 100 years.
    - Alberto Fujimori is removed from office as president of Peru.
- November 27 – Jean Chrétien is re-elected as Prime Minister of Canada, as the Liberal Party of Canada increases its majority in the House of Commons of Canada.
- November 28 – Ukrainian politician Oleksandr Moroz touches off the Cassette Scandal by publicly accusing President Leonid Kuchma of involvement in the murder of journalist Georgiy Gongadze. The accusation creates the Orange Revolution in 2004.

December

- December 1 – Vicente Fox takes office as President of Mexico.
- December 7 – Kadisoka temple discovered in Sleman, Yogyakarta, Indonesia.
- December 12 – *Bush v. Gore*: The U.S. Supreme Court stops the Florida presidential recount, effectively giving the state, and the Presidency, to George W. Bush.
- December 15
    - Disney's Paradise Pier Hotel opens at the Disneyland Resort.
    - The third and final reactor at the Chernobyl Nuclear Power Plant is shut down and the station is shut down completely.
- December 24 – Christmas Eve 2000 Indonesia bombings: 18 people are killed in multiple Islamist bomb attacks on churches across Indonesia.
- December 25 – A shopping center fire at Luoyang, Henan, China, kills 309.
- December 30 – Rizal Day bombings: A series of bombs explode in various places in Metro Manila, Philippines, within a span of a few hours, killing 22 and injuring about 100.
- December 31 – The Millennium Dome closes its doors one year to the day of its opening.

Births

January

Jackie Evancho

- January 8 – Noah Cyrus, American actress

- January 11 - Cho Hee-soo, South Korean figure skater
- January 26
  - Piper Mackenzie Harris, American actress and model
  - Angélique Abachkina,French dancer
- January 30- Isaac Adni English singer and songwriter

February

- February 5– Jordan Nagai, American actor
- February 10 - Yara Shahidi, American actress
- February 21
  - Cho I-hsuan, Taiwanese professional tennis player
  - Yuto Miyazawa - Japanese singer
- February 25
  - Laura Ann Kesling, American actress
  - Tucker Albrizzi, American actor
- February 26 – Alexa Ilacad, Filipina actress

March

- March 2
  - Nahida Akter, Bangladeshi cricketer
  - Julia Kedhammar, Swedish Singer
- March 21 - Jace Norman, American actor
- March 25 – Christian Traeumer, American actor
- March 27 – Sophie Nélisse, Canadian actress
- March 31 – Anu Anand- Indian actress

April

- April 6 – CJ Adams, American actor
- April 7 - Ivan Ivanov (singer) Bulgarian child singer and songwriter.
- April 9 – Jackie Evancho, American soprano
- April 11 – Morgan Lily, American actress
- April 28 – Ellie Carpenter, Australian international footballer

May

- May 7 – Maxwell Perry Cotton, American actor
- May 15 – Jacob Bragg. Australian runner
- May 23 – Evan Bird, Canadian actor
- May 30 – Jared S. Gilmore, American actor

June

Willow Shields

- June 1 – Willow Shields, American actress
- June 5 – Eliias, Swedish singer
- June 16 – Bianca Andreescu,Canadian Tennis player
- June 23
    - Brandon Weaver, American auto racer
    - Kim Hyun-soo. South Korean actress

July

- July 8 – Benjamin Stockham, American actor
- July 16 – Jonathan Morgan Heit, American actor
- July 17
    - Nico Liersch, German actor
    - Maria Aragon, Canadian Singer
- July 24 - Marko Calasan, Macedonian computer systems prodigy
- July 25 – Preston Bailey, American actor
- July 27 – Troy Glass, American actor
- July 28 – Emily Hahn, American actress
- July 29 – Lino Facioli, Brazilian actor

August

- August 3 – Landry Bender, American actress
- August 8 – Félix Auger-Aliassime Canadian junior tennis player
- August 10 – Domina Butic Croatian female water polo player
- August 24 – Griffin Gluck, American actor
- August 25 – Vincenzo Cantiello, Italian Singer
- August 26 – Noah Ryan Scott, Canadian actor
- August 28 – Jaylen Arnold, American activist, philanthropist, and actor

September

- September 5- Ceren Akkaya Turkish Footballer
- September 28
  - Frankie Jonas, American actor
  - Ahn Do-gyu,South Korean actor

October

Connie Talbot

- October 6 – Isobelle Molloy, British actress
- October 10
  - Aedin Mincks, American actor
  - Dima Bashar, Palestinian-Jordanian singer
- October 11 – Hayden Byerly, American actor
- October 15 - David Rawle, Irish actor
- October 31 – Willow Smith, American actress and singer

November

- November 10 – Mackenzie Foy, American model and actress
- November 20 – Connie Talbot, British singer
- November 21 - Megan Roberts, Canadian artistic gymnast

December

- December 12 - Princess Purnika of Nepal, the eldest daughter of Paras, former Crown Prince of Nepal and former Crown Princess of Nepal
- December 24 – Ethan Bortnick, American musician
- December 26 – Isac Elliot, Finnish singer

Deaths

January

Bettino Craxi

Hedy Lamarr

- January 2 – Patrick O'Brian, English writer (b. 1914)

- January 4 - Diether Krebs, German actor, cabaret artist and comedian. (b. 1947)
- January 7 – Gary Albright, American professional wrestler (b. 1963)
- January 8 - Fritz Thiedemann, German equestrian and show jumper (b. 1918)
- January 15 – Željko Ražnatović, Serbian mobster and paramilitary leader (b. 1952)
- January 18 – Frances Drake, American actress (b. 1912)
- January 19
    - Bettino Craxi, Prime Minister of Italy (b. 1934)
    - Hedy Lamarr, Austrian actress (b. 1914)
- January 20 – Izabella Yurieva, Russian singer (b. 1899)
- January 24 – Rex Nelon, American Southern gospel singer (b. 1932)
- January 26 – Don Budge, American tennis player (b. 1915)

February

Doug Henning

Charles M. Schulz

Friedensreich Hundertwasser

- February 5
  - Claude Autant-Lara, French film director (b. 1901)
  - Ward Cornell, Canadian radio/TV broadcaster & educator (b. 1924)
- February 7
  - Doug Henning, Canadian magician (b. 1947)
  - Big Pun, American rapper (b. 1971)
  - Shiho Niiyama, Japanese voice actress (b. 1970)
- February 8
  - Bob Collins, American broadcaster (b. 1942)
  - Sid Abel, Canadian ice hockey player (b. 1918)
  - Derrick Thomas, American football player (b. 1967)
- February 9 – Beau Jack, American boxer (b. 1921)
- February 10 – Jim Varney, American actor noted for his character, Ernest P. Worrell (b. 1949)
- February 11 – Roger Vadim, French film director and producer (b. 1928)
- February 12
  - Tom Landry, American football coach (b. 1924)
  - Charles M. Schulz, American comic strip artist (*Peanuts*) (b. 1922)
  - Oliver, American pop singer (b. 1945)
  - Screamin' Jay Hawkins, African-American rock singer and performer (b. 1929)
- February 13 – Anders Aalborg, Canadian politician (b. 1914)
- February 19 – Friedensreich Hundertwasser, Austrian artist (b. 1928)
- February 23
  - Sir Stanley Matthews, English footballer (b. 1915)
  - Ofra Haza, Israeli singer (b. 1957)
  -

March

Ian Dury

- March 3 – Toni Ortelli, Italian composer and alpinist (b. 1904)
- March 7 – Charles Gray, English actor (b. 1928)
- March 9 – Jean Coulthard, Canadian composer and music educator (b. 1908)
- March 11 – Alfred Schwarzmann, German Olympic gymnast (b. 1912)
- March 27 – Ian Dury, English singer, songwriter (b. 1942)
- March 28 – Anthony Powell, British author (b. 1905)
- March 30 – Rudolf Kirchschläger, former President of Austria (b. 1915)

April

Habib Bourguiba

- April 2 – Tommaso Buscetta, Sicilian mafioso informant (b. 1928)
- April 3 – Terence McKenna, writer, philosopher, writer and entheogen advocate (b. 1946)
- April 4 – Derek Allhusen, British equestrian (b. 1914)
- April 5 – Lee Petty, American race-car driver (b. 1914)
- April 6 – Habib Bourguiba, Tunisian politician, 1st President of Tunisia (b. 1903)
- April 8 – Bernie Grant, British Labour MP (b. 1944)

- April 10
  - Rabah Bitat, former President of Algeria (b. 1925)
  - Larry Linville, American actor (b.1939)
- April 11 – Diana Darvey, British actress, singer and dancer (b. 1945)
- April 14 – Phil Katz, American computer programmer (b. 1962)
- April 15 – Edward Gorey, American writer and illustrator (b. 1925)
- April 25 – David Merrick, American stage producer (b. 1911)
- April 29 – Phạm Văn Đồng, Vietnamese politician, Prime Minister of Vietnam (b. 1906)

May

Douglas Fairbanks, Jr.

Keizō Obuchi

- May 1
  - Steve Reeves, American actor and bodybuilder (b. 1926)
  - Jukka Tapanimäki, Finnish game programmer (b. 1961)
- May 7 – Douglas Fairbanks, Jr., American actor (b. 1909)
- May 8 – Maria do Carmo Gerônimo, The last Brazilian slave who claimed to be 129 before she died (b. 1871)
- May 10
  - Craig Stevens, American actor (b. 1918)

- ○ Kaneto Shiozawa, Japanese voice actor (b. 1954)
- May 11 – René Muñoz, Cuban actor, screenwriter of telenovelas and the cinema of Mexico (b. 1938)
- May 12 – Adam Petty, American NASCAR driver (b. 1980)
- May 13 – Tomomi Tsuruta, Japanese professional wrestler, better known as Jumbo Tsuruta (b. 1951)
- May 14 – Keizō Obuchi, Prime Minister of Japan (b. 1937)
- May 20 – Edward Bernds, American director (b. 1905)
- May 21
  - ○ Dame Barbara Cartland, English novelist (b. 1901)
  - ○ Sir John Gielgud, English actor (b. 1904)
- May 25 – Francis Lederer, film and stage actor (b. 1899)
- May 27
  - ○ Maurice Richard, Canadian hockey player (b. 1921)
  - ○ Kazimierz Leski, Polish engineer, fighter pilot, and Home Army's intelligence and counter-intelligence officer (b. 1912)
  - ○ Erich Mielke, German secret police official (b. 1907)
- May 30 – Doris Hare, English actress, well known for her role in the 1970s comedy *On the Buses* (b. 1905)
- May 31 – Tito Puente, American jazz musician (b. 1923)

June

Hafez al-Assad

- June 10
  - ○ Hafez al-Assad, President of Syria (b. 1930)
  - ○ Frank Patterson, Irish tenor (b. 1938)
- June 14 – Robert Trent Jones, English-born golf course designer (b. 1906)
- June 16 – Empress Kōjun of Japan (b. 1903)

- June 17 – Ismail Mahomed, South African and Namibian Chief Justice (b. 1931)
- June 19 – Noboru Takeshita, former Prime Minister of Japan (b. 1924)
- June 21 – Alan Hovhaness, American composer (b. 1911)
- June 24 – David Tomlinson, English actor (b. 1917)
- June 27 – Pierre Pflimlin, French politician (b. 1907)
- June 29 – Vittorio Gassman, Italian actor (b. 1922)

July

Walter Matthau

- July 1 – Walter Matthau, American actor (b. 1920)
- July 6 – Lazar Koliševski, 2nd President of the Presidency of Yugoslavia (b. 1914)
- July 7 – James C. Quayle, American newspaper publisher (b. 1921)
- July 8 – FM-2030, Transhumanist philosopher (b. 1930)
- July 10
    - Vakkom Majeed, Indian freedom fighter, Travancore-Cochin Legislative member (b. 1909)
    - Denis O'Conor Don, hereditary chief of the O'Conor Don sept of Ireland (b. 1912)
- July 11 – Robert Runcie, Archbishop of Canterbury (b. 1921)
- July 12 – Charles Merritt, Canadian Army officer and recipient of the Victoria Cross during World War II (b. 1908)
- July 15 – Kalle Svensson, Swedish footballer (b. 1925)
- July 21 – Yosef Qafih, Israeli rabbiYemenite Jewish (b. 1917)
- July 28 – Abraham Pais, Dutch-born American physicist (b. 1918)
- July 29 – René Favaloro, Argentinian cardiologist who created the technique for coronary bypass surgery (b. 1923)

August

Sir Alec Guinness

Carl Barks

- August 5
  - Sir Alec Guinness, English actor and writer (b. 1914)
  - Otto Buchsbaum, writer and ecological activist (b. 1920)
- August 6
  - Sir Robin Day, British political broadcaster (b. 1923)
  - Don A. Jones, American admiral and civil engineer, seventh Director of the United States Coast and Geodetic Survey and second Director of the Environmental Science Services Administration Corps (b. 1912)
- August 9 – John Harsanyi, Hungarian-born economist, Nobel Prize laureate (b. 1920)
- August 12
  - Loretta Young, American actress (b. 1913)
  - Dave Edwards, American musician (b. 1941)
- August 13 – Nazia Hassan, Pakistani singer (b. 1964)
- August 19 – Bineshwar Brahma, Bodo activist and leader (b. 1946)
- August 21 – Daniel Lisulo, Zambian politician (b. 1930)
- August 25
  - Ivan Stambolić, Serbian politician (b. 1936)
  - Carl Barks, American cartoonist and screenwriter (b. 1901)

- August 26 – Bunny Austin, English tennis player (b. 1906)

September

Pierre Trudeau

- September 2
  - Elvera Sanchez, American dancer (b. 1905)
  - Curt Siodmak, American novelist and screenwriter (b. 1902)
- September 14 – Beah Richards, American actress (b. 1920)
- September 16 – Georgiy Gongadze, Ukrainian journalist (b. 1969)
- September 19
  - Anthony Robert Klitz, British artist (b. 1917)
  - Ann Doran, American actress (b. 1911)
- September 22 – Saburō Sakai, Japanese fighter ace (b. 1916)
- September 25 – R. S. Thomas, Welsh poet (b. 1913)
- September 26 – Richard Mulligan, American actor (b. 1932)
- September 27 – Sammy Luftspring, Canadian boxer (b. 1916)
- September 28
  - Peter Gennaro, American dancer and choreographer (b. 1919)
  - Pierre Trudeau, 15th Prime Minister of Canada (b. 1919)

October

Rodney Anoa'i

Steve Allen

- October 3 – Benjamin Orr, American singer-songwriter, guitarist and singer for the band The Cars (b. 1947)
- October 4 – Michael Smith, English-born chemist, Nobel Prize laureate (b. 1932)
- October 6 – Richard Farnsworth, American actor (b. 1920)
- October 7 – Walter Krupinski, German World War II fighter ace and postwar general (b. 1920)
- October 8 – Sheila Holland (Sheila Coates, Charlotte Lamb, Sheila Lancaster, Victoria Wolf, Laura Hardy), English writer (b. 1937)
- October 9 – Patrick Anthony Porteous, Scottish recipient of the Victoria Cross (b. 1918)
- October 13 – Jean Peters, American actress (b. 1926)
- October 14 – Tony Roper, American NASCAR driver (b. 1964)
- October 15 – Konrad Emil Bloch, German-born biochemist, recipient of the Nobel Prize in Physiology or Medicine (b. 1912)
- October 16 – Mel Carnahan, American politician and former Governor of Missouri (b. 1934)
- October 18 – Julie London, American singer and actress (b. 1926)
- October 19 - Charles Perkins, Australian Aboriginal activist and Soccer player (b. 1936)
- October 21 – Reginald Kray, leading figure in organised crime in London, UK (b. 1933)
- October 23 – Rodney Anoa'i, American wrestler known as Yokozuna (b. 1966)
- October 27 – Walter Berry, Austrian bass-baritone (b. 1929)
- October 29 – Andújar Cedeño, Dominican Major League Baseball player for the Houston Astros (b. 1969)

- October 30 – Steve Allen, American comedian, composer, talk show host, and author (b. 1921)
- October 31 – Ring Lardner, Jr., American screenwriter, one of the Hollywood Ten (b. 1915)

November

Ingrid of Sweden

- November 2 – Eva Morris, last surviving person documented as born in 1885 (b. 1885)
- November 5
  - David Brower, American environmental activist (b. 1912)
  - Jimmie Davis, American singer (b. 1899)
  - Roger Peyrefitte, French writer and diplomat (b. 1907)
- November 6 – L. Sprague de Camp, American writer (b. 1907)
- November 7
  - C Subramaniam, Indian politician (b. 1910)
  - Ingrid of Sweden, Queen consort of Frederick IX of Denmark (b. 1910)
- November 11 – Hugh Paddick, British actor (b. 1915)
- November 16 – DJ Screw, American hip hop DJ (b. 1971)
- November 22
  - Sir Cyril Astley Clarke, British physician, geneticist and entomologist, former President of the Royal College of Physicians (b. 1907)
  - Christian Marquand, French actor and director (b. 1927)
- November 28 – Liane Haid, Austrian actress (b. 1895)

December

- December 2 – Gail Fisher, American actress (b. 1935)

- December 3 – Gwendolyn Brooks, African American-writer (b. 1917)
- December 6 – Werner Klemperer, German born American actor (Hogan's Heroes) (b. 1920)
- December 10
    - Paul Avery, American journalist (b. 1934)
    - Marie Windsor, American actress (b. 1919)
- December 18 – Kirsty MacColl, English singer (b. 1959)
- December 19 – Roebuck "Pops" Staples, patriarch of The Staple Singers (b. 1914)
- December 23
    - Billy Barty, American actor (b. 1924)
    - Victor Borge, Danish-born comedian and pianist (b. 1909)
- December 26 – Jason Robards, American actor (b. 1922)
- December 30 – Julius J. Epstein, American screenwriter (b. 1909)

Nobel Prizes

- Chemistry – Alan J. Heeger, Alan MacDiarmid, and Hideki Shirakawa
- Economics – James Heckman and Daniel McFadden
- Literature – Gao Xingjian
- Peace – Kim Dae-jung
- Physics – Zhores Alferov, Herbert Kroemer, and Jack Kilby
- Physiology or Medicine – Arvid Carlsson, Paul Greengard, and Eric Kandel

In the News

The Tate Modern opens in London.

Divers discover the ancient port of Alexandria the home of Cleopatra and Mark Anthony.

Sony releases the Playstation 2 Gaming Console in Japan.

Mad Cow Disease causes alarm in Europe due to it's growth.

The Summer Olympics are held in Sydney Australia.

Tiger Woods becomes the youngest player to win a Grand Slam in Golf.

Microsoft releases Windows 2000.

The Latest Harry Potter Book Is Published "Harry Potter and the Goblet of Fire"

Popular Films - How the Grinch Stole Christmas!, Cast Away, Mission: Impossible II, Gladiator.

2000 Calendar

January 2000
Sun	Mon	Tue	Wed	Thu	Fri	Sat
						1
2	3	4	5	6	7	8
9	10	11	12	13	14	15
16	17	18	19	20	21	22
23	24	25	26	27	28	29
30	31					

February 2000
Sun	Mon	Tue	Wed	Thu	Fri	Sat
		1	2	3	4	5
6	7	8	9	10	11	12
13	14	15	16	17	18	19
20	21	22	23	24	25	26
27	28	29				

March 2000
Sun	Mon	Tue	Wed	Thu	Fri	Sat
			1	2	3	4
5	6	7	8	9	10	11
12	13	14	15	16	17	18
19	20	21	22	23	24	25
26	27	28	29	30	31	

April 2000
Sun	Mon	Tue	Wed	Thu	Fri	Sat
						1
2	3	4	5	6	7	8
9	10	11	12	13	14	15
16	17	18	19	20	21	22
23	24	25	26	27	28	29
30						

May 2000
Sun	Mon	Tue	Wed	Thu	Fri	Sat
	1	2	3	4	5	6
7	8	9	10	11	12	13
14	15	16	17	18	19	20
21	22	23	24	25	26	27
28	29	30	31			

June 2000
Sun	Mon	Tue	Wed	Thu	Fri	Sat
				1	2	3
4	5	6	7	8	9	10
11	12	13	14	15	16	17
18	19	20	21	22	23	24
25	26	27	28	29	30	

July 2000
Sun	Mon	Tue	Wed	Thu	Fri	Sat
						1
2	3	4	5	6	7	8
9	10	11	12	13	14	15
16	17	18	19	20	21	22
23	24	25	26	27	28	29
30	31					

August 2000
Sun	Mon	Tue	Wed	Thu	Fri	Sat
		1	2	3	4	5
6	7	8	9	10	11	12
13	14	15	16	17	18	19
20	21	22	23	24	25	26
27	28	29	30	31		

September 2000
Sun	Mon	Tue	Wed	Thu	Fri	Sat
					1	2
3	4	5	6	7	8	9
10	11	12	13	14	15	16
17	18	19	20	21	22	23
24	25	26	27	28	29	30

October 2000
Sun	Mon	Tue	Wed	Thu	Fri	Sat
1	2	3	4	5	6	7
8	9	10	11	12	13	14
15	16	17	18	19	20	21
22	23	24	25	26	27	28
29	30	31				

November 2000
Sun	Mon	Tue	Wed	Thu	Fri	Sat
			1	2	3	4
5	6	7	8	9	10	11
12	13	14	15	16	17	18
19	20	21	22	23	24	25
26	27	28	29	30		

December 2000
Sun	Mon	Tue	Wed	Thu	Fri	Sat
					1	2
3	4	5	6	7	8	9
10	11	12	13	14	15	16
17	18	19	20	21	22	23
24	25	26	27	28	29	30
31